FACT CAT

RUSSIA

Izzi Howell

WAYLAND
www.waylandbooks.co.uk

FACT CAT

Get your paws on this fantastic new mega-series from Wayland!

Join our Fact Cat on a journey of fun learning about every subject under the sun!

First published in Great Britain in 2017 by Wayland
Copyright © Hodder and Stoughton Limited, 2017

ISBN: 978 1 5263 0363 9

10 9 8 7 6 5 4 3 2 1

MIX
Paper from responsible sources
FSC® C104740

Wayland
An imprint of Hachette Children's Group
Part of Hodder & Stoughton
Carmelite House
50 Victoria Embankment
London EC4Y 0DZ

An Hachette UK Company
www.hachette.co.uk
www.hachettechildrens.co.uk

A catalogue for this title is available from
the British Library
Printed and bound in China

Produced for Wayland by
White-Thomson Publishing Ltd
www.wtpub.co.uk

Editor: Izzi Howell
Design: Clare Nicholas
Fact Cat illustrations: Shutterstock/Julien Troneur
Other illustrations: Stefan Chabluk
Consultant: Karina Philip

Picture and illustration credits:
Alamy: Greek photonews 20, ITAR-TASS Photo Agency 21;
iStock: JavenLin 6, Sergey_Krasnoshchokov 13t, Kai_Wong 15t, Shutterstock: Grisha Bruev cover, Iakov Filimonov title page and 16b, Palette7 5l, walter_g 5r, Brian Kinney 7, rtem 8t, toiletroom 8-9, V. Smirnov 10, Katvic 11t, S-F 11b, Vadim Petrakov 12, S.R. Maglione 13bl, Victor Tyakht 13br, yamix 14, vladimir salman 15b, V. Smirnov 16t, Marianna Ianovska 17, Idea Studio 18, Iurii Osadchi 19.
Should there be any inadvertent omission, please apply to the publisher for rectification.

FACT CAT FACT

There is a question for you to answer on most spreads in this book. You can check your answers on page 24.

CONTENTS

Welcome to Russia.............4

Cities.......................6

Countryside...................8

Coasts, lakes and rivers......10

Wildlife.....................12

Food........................14

Festivals....................16

Sport........................18

Famous people................20

Quiz.........................22

Glossary.....................23

Index........................24

Answers......................24

WELCOME TO RUSSIA

Russia is a country in Europe and Asia. It is the largest country in the world. Over 142 million people live in Russia.

Russia shares a border with fourteen countries in two different **continents**. Look at the map and name three countries that share a border with Russia.

FACT CAT FACT

Russia covers the same area as all the land on the planet Pluto.

USA

Bering Sea

Arctic Ocean

ASIA

NORWAY

SWEDEN

FINLAND

ESTONIA

LITHUANIA

LATVIA

RUSSIA

St Petersburg

BELARUS

Moscow

River Volga

UKRAINE

Perm

Samara

Omsk

Novosibirsk

SIBERIA

River Lena

RUSSIA

Lake Baikal

Vladivostok

CHINA

Sochi

Caspian Sea

KAZAKHSTAN

MONGOLIA

NORTH KOREA

GEORGIA

AZERBAIJAN

IRAQ

UZBEKISTAN

TURKMENISTAN

KYRGYZSTAN

SOUTH KOREA

IRAN

Many beautiful crafts are made in Russia, such as wooden matryoshka dolls that fit inside each other. Fabergé eggs are made from expensive metal and jewels.

This Fabergé egg is decorated with pictures of Russian kings and queens.

Matryoshka dolls are painted so that they look like they are wearing **traditional** Russian clothes.

CITIES

Most people in Russia live in cities. Moscow is the **capital** city of Russia. Over 12 million people live there. It has many old, beautiful buildings.

St Basil's Cathedral in Moscow is decorated with colourful designs.

Saint Petersburg is the second largest city, after Moscow. It is on the northwest coast of Russia.

In the past, the emperors of Russia lived in the Winter Palace in Saint Petersburg. Today, it is a museum.

FACT CAT FACT

There are 1,500 rooms and 117 staircases in the Winter Palace!

COUNTRYSIDE

There are several high **mountain ranges** in Russia. The Ural Mountains are in the west of Russia. They run from the north to the south of the country.

The Caucasus Mountains are in the southwest of Russia. The tops of the mountains are often covered in snow.

The south of Russia is covered in **grasslands** called steppes. There are large areas of forest to the north of the steppes. At the very north of Russia, the countryside is rocky with no trees.

FACT CAT FACT

The Trans-Siberian Railway goes from the west to the far east of Russia, through many different landscapes. Here, it is going through the grassy steppes.

The Trans-Siberian Railway is the longest railway in the world! It takes over 6 days to travel from Moscow in the west to Vladivostok in the east. How long is the railway in kilometres?

COASTS, LAKES AND RIVERS

Russia has a long coastline along the Arctic and Pacific Oceans. The **climate** on the north coast of Russia is very cold. The sea often freezes into **ice**.

Sochi is a Russian city on the coast of the Black Sea. It has a **tropical** climate. Many people visit Sochi for a holiday.

There are thousands of rivers and lakes in Russia. Ships transport **goods** around Russia by river. Some rivers have **dams** that make electricity.

Lake Baikal is a large lake in the east of Russia. It is known for its wildlife and clear, clean water. Find out the name of an animal that lives in Lake Baikal.

FACT CAT FACT

Lake Baikal is the deepest lake in the world. In some places, the **distance** from the bottom of the lake to the **surface** is the same as twice the height of the tallest building on Earth, the Burj Khalifa!

830m

WILDLIFE

Different animals live in each area of the Russian countryside. **Herbivores**, such as deer and rabbits, live on the grassy steppes. Squirrels and **lynx** live in the forests.

Brown bears live in forests across Russia. They are often used as a **symbol** of Russia.

Only a few animals can **survive** the freezing weather in northern Russia. Many animals, such as the arctic fox, have thick fur to keep them warm.

Reindeer dig in the snow with their **hooves** to find plants to eat.

FACT CAT FACT

Russia is home to **endangered** animals, such as the Siberian tiger and the saiga antelope. In which part of Russia does the Siberian tiger live?

FOOD

Many Russian dishes are made from ingredients that grow well in cold Russian weather, such as beetroot, cabbage and potatoes. They add meat to these vegetables to make soups and stews.

Borscht is a traditional Russian soup. Which vegetable is it made from?

Russians eat many types of sweet and **savoury** pastries, called pirogi. Sweet pirogi have fruit, honey or nuts inside.

This is a savoury pirogi, called a coulibiac (say cool-ee-bee-ack). It has mushrooms, rice and salmon inside.

FACT CAT FACT

In Russia, tea is traditionally made in a large metal container called a **samovar**. People add sugar, lemon or jam to their tea before drinking it!

FESTIVALS

Maslenitsa is a Russian religious holiday that takes place in the spring. During the week of Maslenitsa, people eat thin pancakes called blini and make large dolls out of straw.

These people are dancing around their Maslenitsa doll. Later, they will set their doll on fire.

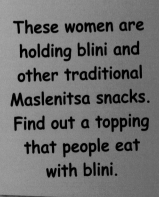

These women are holding blini and other traditional Maslenitsa snacks. Find out a topping that people eat with blini.

Every year, the city of Saint Petersburg holds a massive festival called the White Nights Festival. There are concerts, parades and carnivals.

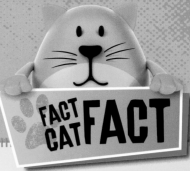

The White Nights festival celebrates the light nights of summer in Russia. During the summer, the sun almost never sets.

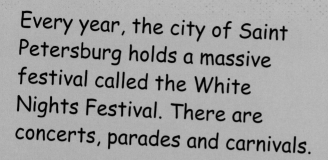

More than a million people come to watch the fireworks and boat races in the Scarlet Sails show, which takes place during the White Nights festival.

SPORT

Ice hockey is one of the most popular sports in Russia. People enjoy watching professional ice hockey teams from across Russia and Europe play together in a **league**.

Many Russians enjoy the sport of bandy, which is a type of ice hockey played with a ball.

Many important sporting events have taken place in Russia. In 1980, the Summer Olympics were held in Moscow. In 2014, the Winter Olympics took place in Sochi.

Skiing was one of the many winter sports events at the Sochi Winter Olympics. Find out the name of another Winter Olympic sport.

FACT CAT FACT

Since the beginning of the Olympics, Russia has won over 1,200 Olympic medals!

FAMOUS PEOPLE

Garry Kasparov is a **retired** chess player from Russia. In the past, he won many competitions. Many people think that he is the best chess player of all time.

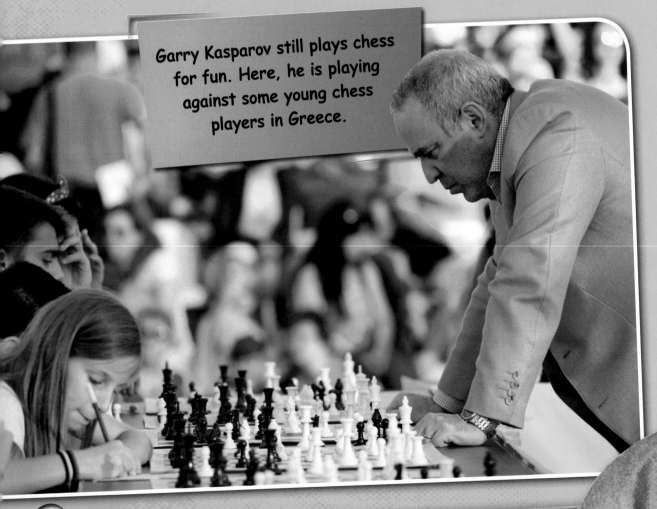

Garry Kasparov still plays chess for fun. Here, he is playing against some young chess players in Greece.

Some of the most important cosmonauts (astronauts) of all time came from Russia. In 1961, Yuri Gagarin was the first person to travel into space. Valentina Tereshkova was the first woman in space in 1963.

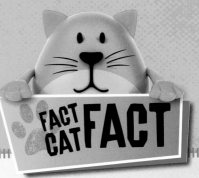

FACT CAT FACT

Valentina Tereshkova spent three days in space. How many times did she orbit (circle) the Earth?

Yuri Gagarin spent 108 minutes in space, circling the Earth once in his spaceship, *Vostok 1.*

21

QUIZ

Try to answer the questions below. Look back through the book to help you. Check your answers on page 24.

1 Russia is the largest country in the world. True or not true?

a) true

b) not true

2 What is the capital city of Russia?

a) Sochi

b) Saint Petersburg

c) Moscow

3 Which Russian animal is endangered?

a) Siberian tiger

b) reindeer

c) brown bear

4 Maslenitsa takes place in autumn. True or not true?

a) true

b) not true

5 The 2014 Winter Olympics were held in Moscow. True or not true?

a) true

b) not true

6 In which year did Yuri Gagarin travel into space?

a) 1958

b) 1961

c) 1963

GLOSSARY

border a line that separates two countries

capital the city where a government meets to make the laws of a country

climate the weather in an area

continent one of the seven large areas of land on Earth, such as Africa and Asia

dam a wall built across a river that collects the water and can use it to make electricity

distance the amount of space between two places

emperor a ruler

endangered describes an animal or plant that may soon not exist because there are not many of them left alive

goods objects that will be sold

grassland an area of land covered in grass with very few trees

herbivore an animal that only eats plants

hooves the hard feet of a reindeer or horse

ice frozen water

league a group of sports teams who take part in competitions between each other

lynx a wild type of cat

mountain range a group of mountains

retired describes someone who has stopped working, often because of age

samovar a large metal container used to make tea

savoury salty or spicy, not sweet

surface the top part of something

survive to stay alive

symbol something that is used to represent something else

traditional the way that people have done things for a long time

tropical describes warm weather

23

INDEX

animals 11, 12-13

border 4

climate 10, 13, 14
coasts 10

Fabergé eggs 5
food 14–15, 16
forests 9, 12

Gagarin, Yuri 21

ice hockey 18

Kasparov, Garry 20

Lake Baikal 11

Maslenitsa 16
matryoshka dolls 5
Moscow 6, 9
mountains 8

Olympics 19

Saint Petersburg 7, 17
Sochi 10, 19
steppes 9, 12

tea 15
Tereshkova, Valentina 21
Trans-Siberian Railway 9

White Nights Festival 17

ANSWERS

Pages 4–21

Page 4: Some countries include Norway, Georgia and China.

Page 9: 9,289 kilometres

Page 11: Some animals include the Baikal seal, sturgeon and the oilfish.

Page 13: The east coast of Russia

Page 14: Beetroot

Page 16: Some common toppings include fish and jam.

Page 19: Some sports include ice skating and bobsleigh.

Page 21: 48 times

Quiz answers

1   true

2   c – Moscow

3   a – Siberian tiger

4   not true – it takes place in spring.

5   not true – they were held in Sochi.

6   b – 1961

OTHER TITLES IN THE FACT CAT SERIES...

Space
The Earth 978 0 7502 8220 8
The Moon 978 0 7502 8221 5
The Planets 978 0 7502 8222 2
The Sun 978 0 7502 8223 9

United Kingdom
England 978 0 7502 8927 6
Northern Ireland 978 0 7502 8942 9
Scotland 978 0 7502 8928 3
Wales 978 0 7502 8943 6

Countries
Brazil 978 0 7502 8213 0
France 978 0 7502 8212 3
Ghana 978 0 7502 8215 4
Italy 978 0 7502 8214 7
Russia 978 1 5263 0363 9

Habitats
Ocean 978 0 7502 8218 5
Rainforest 978 0 7502 8219 2
Seashore 978 0 7502 8216 1
Woodland 978 0 7502 8217 8

History
Neil Armstrong 978 0 7502 9040 1
Amelia Earhart 978 0 7502 9034 0
Christopher Columbus 978 0 7502 9031 9
The Wright Brothers 978 0 7502 9037 1
Edith Cavell 978 0 7502 9772 1
Emily Davison 978 0 7502 9770 7
Mary Seacole 978 0 7502 9854 4
Rosa Parks 978 0 7502 9771 4
Florence Nightingale 978 1 5263 0168 0
Samuel Pepys 978 1 5263 0097 3

Early Britons
Anglo-Saxons 978 0 7502 9579 6
Roman Britain 978 0 7502 9582 6
Stone Age to Iron Age 978 0 7502 9580 2
Vikings 978 0 7502 9581 9

Animals
Mammals 978 0 7502 9598 7
Reptiles 978 0 7502 9602 1
Amphibians 978 0 7502 9599 4
Birds 978 0 7502 9601 4
Fish 978 0 7502 9600 7

Geography
Continents 978 0 7502 9025 8
The Equator 978 0 7502 9019 7
The Poles 978 0 7502 9022 7
Seas and Oceans 978 0 7502 9028 9

Science
Food Chains 978 0 7502 9695 3
Seasons 978 0 7502 9696 0
The Water Cycle 978 0 7502 9694 6
Weather 978 0 7502 9693 9
Electricity 978 1 5263 0178 9
Forces and Magnets 978 1 5263 0172 7
Light 978 1 5263 0174 1
Materials 978 1 5263 0170 3
Plants 978 1 5263 0099 7
Sound 978 1 5263 0176 5

WAYLAND
www.waylandbooks.co.uk